£7.25

ALLOW ME TO HELP, DEAR LADY. IT WILL BE MY PLEASURE TO MENACEPROOF YOUR HOUSE.

OO! YOU'RE SUCH A SWEET CHILD, WALTER!

So, later—

TIME TO HEAD DOWN STAIRS AGAIN, MENACE-STYLE.

TEE-HEE! FIRST I STICK THIS VELCRO PAD ON THE BANISTER...

And—

STICK!

W-WOW!

THE BRACELET IS ACTUALLY A TRACKING DEVICE. WHEN I SWITCH IT ON, I CAN TELL WHEN GEEKY-BOY IS GETTING TOO CLOSE TO ME - THEN I SCARPER - SHARPISH!

BREEP! BREEP! BREEP!

CLICK!

LATER...

IT'S SHOP TILL I DROP DAY! I'LL SWITCH ON TO MAKE SURE ERNEST'S NOT ANYWHERE NEAR ME.

BREEP! BREEP! BREEP! BREEP! BREEP!

BLING AND BLING JEWELLERS

OPEN

ERK! NEAR ME? HE'S ALMOST RIGHT BESIDE ME! I'VE GOTTA GET OUTA HERE - FAST!

MY TRACKING DEVICE WORKED - SO FEET, DON'T FAIL ME NOW!

ZOOM!

BUT...

SPLOM!

YEE-HAW, YAH-HOO AN' YAH-BOY, SIR! THAT WAS GRRRRRRRRRRRRRREAT! PLEASE, MISTER ARTIST - DO A SLOW MOTION OF THAT LAST PICTURE FOR ME - PRETTY, PRETTY, PRETTY PLEASE!

OKAY, ERNEST. BRACE YOURSELF - HERE IT IS VERY S-L-O-W-L-Y!

M-U-S-T R-U-N!

OH...

...NO...

...NOT...

...THIS!

MMMPH!

WE DIDDIT! WE DID A KISSY-WISSY! DEEP JOY!

GAG! B-BUT HOW? HEY! YOU'RE NOT WEARING THE B-BRACELET!

I KNOW! I PUT IT INTO BLING AND BLING'S, THE JEWELLERS', TO HAVE A LINK TAKEN OUT SO IT WOULD FIT ME BETTER! I DIDN'T WANT TO LOSE IT.

STUPID ERNEST? STUPID PLAN! STUPID BRACELET! STUPID, STUPID, STUPID DAISY!

BAM! BAM! BAM!

DAISY'S LOST IT - BIG TIME!

Rhyme Time

Beano characters show they are not averse to a verse!

A lemming by name Alexander,
Once borrowed an
electric sander.
Our chum switched it on,
Then VOOM! — it was gone!
It took him to far
off Uganda!

A naughty young
girlie named Bea,
Decided to climb up a tree.
She was so happy,
She threw off her nappy,
Which fell on a Softy
— TEE-HEE!

A Beanotown schoolkid
named Plug,
Had a totally hideous mug.
But what do you know,
At the local dog show,
He was chased by an
amorous pug.

WHAT'S HE UP TO?

LOOK AT THAT! WHO IS THIS GUY?

HE MUST BE SOME KIND OF ATHLETE!

MAYBE. BUT I WONDER...

HUH? WHERE DID HE GO?

THERE HE IS! LOOK AT HIM MOVE!

HE'S FAST ALL RIGHT!

CONTINUED LATER IN THIS ANNUAL

LITTLE PLUM

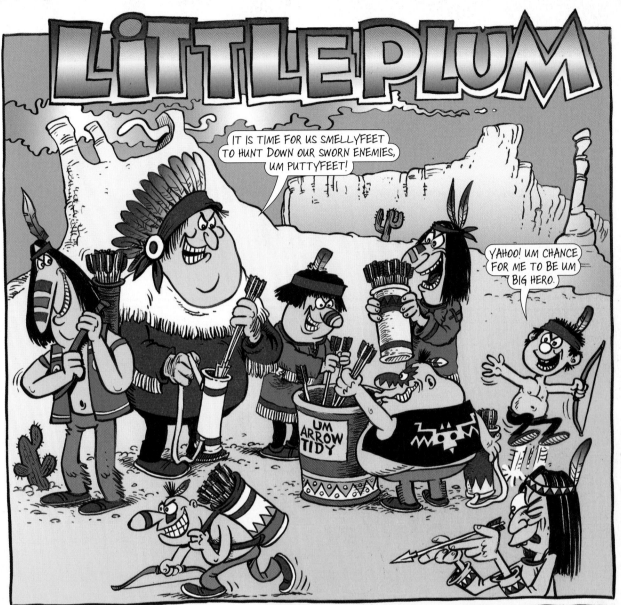

But—

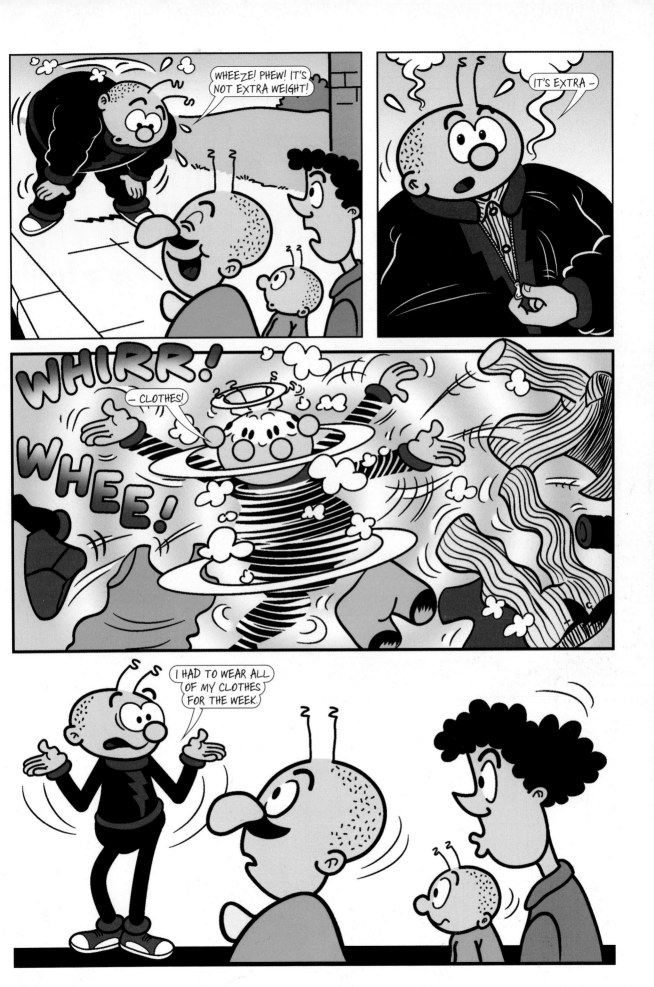

DEREK the SHEEP

Bit chilly out here in the field today.

Fortuntely, me 'n' the lads have these toasty warm fleeces to keep us nice 'n' cosy.

Munch!

Baa!

Right! Come on, Cyril! Time to round up 'em stupid sheep for shearing.

Ruff!

ºScoot!!

Flippin' 'eck!

Ruff! Bow! Yap!

Arf! Ruff!

'Ere, Lenny! You speak 'Sheepdog' — what's he saying?

He's saying, "Get in that pen or I'll bite yer bums."

Charming!

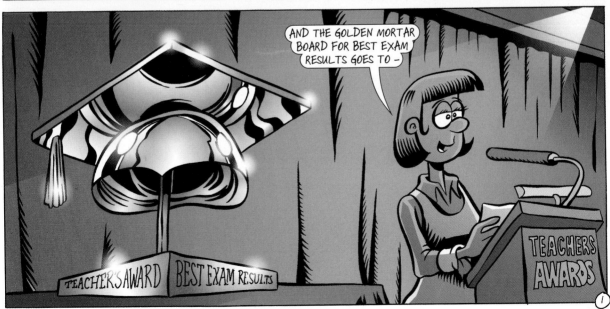

ST. POSHO'S!

CLAP CLAP CLAP CLAP CLAP CLAP

AGAIN. OH THIS IS RUBBISH. WE NEVER WIN ANYTHING.

I KNOW. THE ONLY WAY WE'D WIN ANYTHING IS IF THEY INVENTED A SPECIAL CATEGORY LIKE –

THE SPECIAL AWARD FOR THE SCHOOL THAT SURVIVES HAVING THE WORST PUPILS ON THE PLANET, GOES TO –

BA –

And the winner is (OH NO!) Bash Street

SNATCH

OH YOU SHOULDN'T! YOU'RE TOO KIND!

LOVES! DARLINGS! MWAH! MWAH!

BASH STREET ACCEPTS THIS GOLDEN MORTAR BOARD WITH PRIDE AND HUMBLE DIGNITY.

CONGRATULATIONS, CHAPS, I'D JUST LIKE TO SAY –

WHATEVER!

LOSER!

WE WON A PRIZE! WE WON A PRIZE! WE WON WE WON WE WON A PRIZE!!

2

WHAT IS A MORTAR BOARD FOR?

YOU SHOULD KNOW, YOU WEAR ONE!

I MEAN, A TINY CAP WITH A FLAT BIT ON TOP? WHAT ARE YOU SUPPOSED TO DO WITH THAT?

SEVEN, EIGHT.... NINE ... GO ON, ONE MORE, YOU CAN DO IT!

SO CHILDREN, THAT IS WHY WE ARE SO PROUD OF OUR NEW GOLDEN MORTAR BOARD.

AND THIS AFTERNOON I SHALL BE PLACING IT IN OUR TROPHY CABINET –

ER ... HEADMASTER ...

AND THIS AFTERNOON I SHALL BE BUYING A TROPHY CABINET.

YOU DON'T THINK THAT'S A BIT TOO BIG?

NOT AT ALL!

TROPHY CABINETS 'R' US

EXTRA LARGE

MEDIUM

SMALL

THE GOLDEN MORTAR BOARD IS THE FIRST OF MANY! NEXT WE SHALL WIN SPORTING PRIZES AND –

3

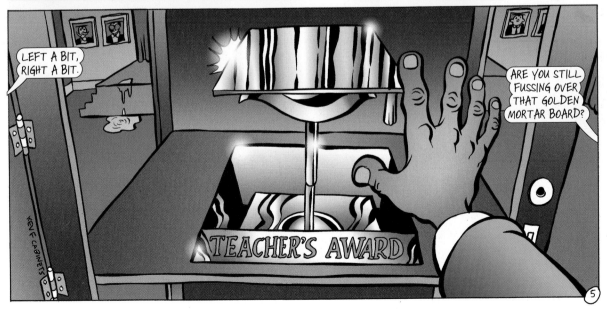

AND SO, A FEW NIGHTS LATER –

SIR, THE PARENTS ARE ARRIVING.

ALREADY?

SORRY, HEAD, THE WORLD RECORD WILL HAVE TO WAIT.

YES! I MUST GO AND GREET THEM!

ER, YOU COULDN'T GIVE ME A HAND WITH THESE BOOKS?

PARENTS EVENING

CRASH! CLATTER THUD BREAK! OUCH!!

TROPHIES

OUR FIRST PRIZE AWARD

WHAT, THIS LITTLE THING? I'D TOTALLY FORGOTTEN IT WAS THERE.

PARENTS EVENIN

SHALL I LET THEM IN?

WHEN YOU'RE READY.

Q HERE

PLEASE TRY TO REMEMBER YOUR CHILD'S NAME

I'VE LEARNT SOME LESSONS FROM THAT TV CHEF GORDON RAMSAY.

FINGER FOOD   TUCK IN

SPROUT SANDWICHES? CUSTARD-ON-STICKS? DOESN'T LOOK LIKE GORDON RAMSAY'S FOOD.

FINGER FOOD   TUCK IN

NO, BUT I SAID A LOT OF SWEARY WORDS WHILE I MADE IT.

FINGER FOOD   TUCK IN

11

AH, YOU MUST BE CUTHBERT'S FATHER?

I FIND CUTHBERT'S WORK VERY GOOD, DON'T YOU?

HE'S GOING TO DO WELL IN HIS EXAMS, ISN'T HE?

MATHS - GOOD, ART - GOOD, ENGLISH - GOOD. TOP MARKS ALL ROUND.

WELL, NICE TO TALK TO YOU.

YOU, TOO.

MR. FATTY, I SAID I WAS TEACHING HIM ABOUT 'PI'!

YES, THE TWINS FIGHT A LITTLE AT HOME, BUT WE CAN HANDLE IT ...

D'YOU KNOW WE THINK THE LAD'S SPOTS WILL CLEAR UP ANY DAY NOW.

WELL, IF THAT'S EVERYTHING, I'LL SEE YOU SAME TIME NEXT YEAR.

PHEW! AM I GLAD THAT'S OVER.

ME, TOO. I'M WORKED OFF MY FEET.

WHAT DO YOU MEAN? YOU'VE JUST BEEN STANDING THERE ALL NIGHT SAYING –

– "HAVE YOU SEEN OUR GOLDEN MORTARBOARD?"

HAVE YOU SEEN OUR GOLDEN MORTAR BOARD?

SEE, EXACTLY LIKE THAT. NOT DIFFICULT, IS IT?

NO – HAVE YOU SEEN OUR GOLDEN MORTAR BOARD?

OKAY, YOU CAN STOP NOW. THEY'VE ALL GONE ...

NO ... HAVE YOU SEEN OUR G – G – G – G –

AAAAARGH!

BASH STREET SCHOOL

TWINNED WITH ASTERIX ECOLE

13

14

15

DENNIS'S MUM IN ...
AN ALIEN CAME TO TEA!

COO-EE! Dennis's Mum here! The other day I was in the sitting-room having a nice cup of tea and a lemon tart while I watched daytime TV. Well, would you believe it, suddenly an intense white light filled the room and I nearly choked on my home baking.

Next thing you know, a warty Alien with six eyes and two long tentacles materialises in front of me. A lovely shade of purple he was – just like the curtains in the spare room or the colour Dad's face goes when he hears about little scamp, Dennis's latest prank. Anyway, this Alien, Morzog his name was, from the Planet Ming, says he needs to find out everything I know about the folks in Beanotown, just in case his planet fancied a spot of World Domination. By the way, he had a lovely speaking voice for a creature whose mouth was on its bottom.

Once he'd shoved a few of my tarts up his backside, he switched on his vacuum-cleaner tentacle. I thought that he was going to clear up all the tart crumbs, but no – he stuck the nozzle against my forehead and pressed the 'Read' button. Ever such a clever gizmo it turned out to be – sucked up all the information that was in my brain. I don't think he got what he wanted, though. My mind's full of info about Coronation Street, EastEnders, Emmerdale and the like but not much else. Well, Soaps are what life's all about, aren't they?

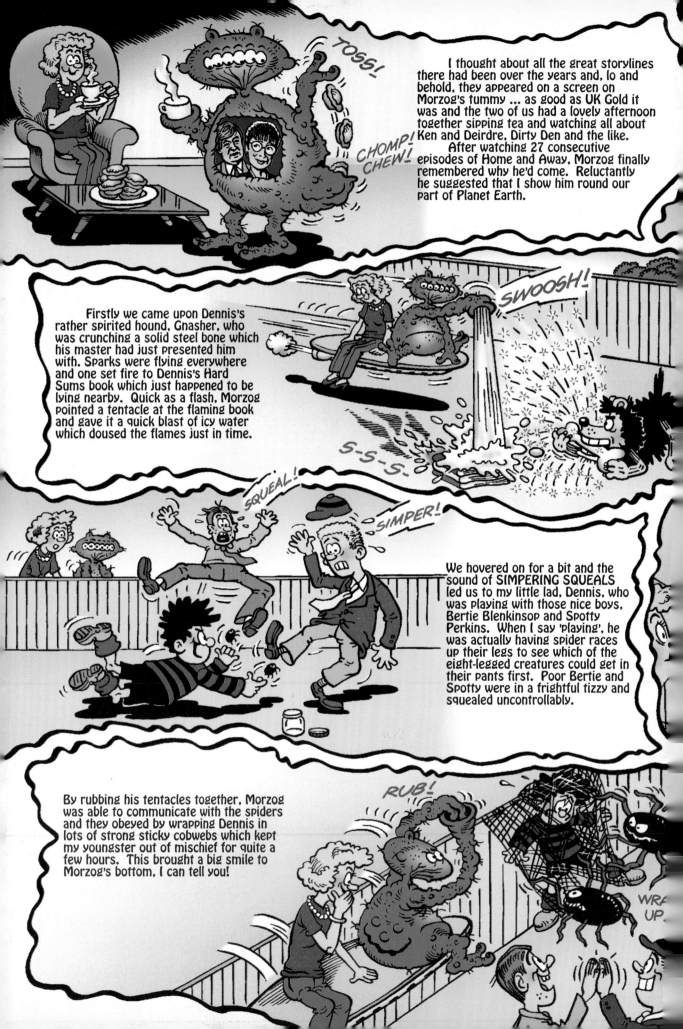

TOSS!

CHOMP! CHEW!

I thought about all the great storylines there had been over the years and, lo and behold, they appeared on a screen on Morzog's tummy ... as good as UK Gold it was and the two of us had a lovely afternoon together sipping tea and watching all about Ken and Deirdre, Dirty Den and the like.

After watching 27 consecutive episodes of Home and Away, Morzog finally remembered why he'd come. Reluctantly he suggested that I show him round our part of Planet Earth.

SWOOSH!

S-S-S.

Firstly we came upon Dennis's rather spirited hound, Gnasher, who was crunching a solid steel bone which his master had just presented him with. Sparks were flying everywhere and one set fire to Dennis's Hard Sums book which just happened to be lying nearby. Quick as a flash, Morzog pointed a tentacle at the flaming book and gave it a quick blast of icy water which doused the flames just in time.

SQUEAL!

SIMPER!

We hovered on for a bit and the sound of SIMPERING SQUEALS led us to my little lad, Dennis, who was playing with those nice boys, Bertie Blenkinsop and Spotty Perkins. When I say 'playing', he was actually having spider races up their legs to see which of the eight-legged creatures could get in their pants first. Poor Bertie and Spotty were in a frightful tizzy and squealed uncontrollably.

RUB!

WRAP UP!

By rubbing his tentacles together, Morzog was able to communicate with the spiders and they obeyed by wrapping Dennis in lots of strong sticky cobwebs which kept my youngster out of mischief for quite a few hours. This brought a big smile to Morzog's bottom, I can tell you!

He snapped his toes (he didn't have fingers, you see) and in whisked a hoverboard. "What do you think of that?" he asked and I replied by ironing three of Dad's shirts on the board. Morzog explained that it wasn't an ironing board but a means of transport and we both jumped aboard and headed off to see the good citizens of Beanotown – and the BAD citizens of Beanotown, come to that.

SNAP!

IRON!

Gnasher seemed a bit put out by this and snarled menacingly at my little Alien chum. Before the naughty doggie could lay a tooth on my purple pal, another high pressure blast of water sent the dastardly doggie spinning over the nearest fence.

SWOOSH!

BLAST!

They passed out completely when Morzog sent a ray from another of his tentacles at the hairy little horrors (that's the spiders, not Dennis). Suddenly the arachnids (that's the posh name for spiders I learned from 'Who Wants to be a Millionaire'), grew to 20 times their normal size.

PZZ!

GROW!

Further on the sweet trill of a boy soprano's voice filled the air and we looked over a nearby fence hedge to see that delightful Walter spraying extra perfume on the pretty flowers in his garden, while he sang snatches of light opera.

IN AN ENGLISH COUNTRY GARDEN!

DUST!

SPRAY!

He busied himself removing any specks of dirt from the blooms with a large, colourful feather duster.

DUST!

Now it just so happened that a cobweb or two had attached themselves to Morzog's tentacles. Quick as a flash, Walter flicked his feather duster all over my new friend.

Would you believe it, the poor alien collapsed in a heap, cackling like a pack of hyenas watching 'Only Fools and Horses'. He just lay there giggling, guffawing, chuckling, chortling, tittering and hooting for close on half-an-hour.

SPIN!

ROLL!

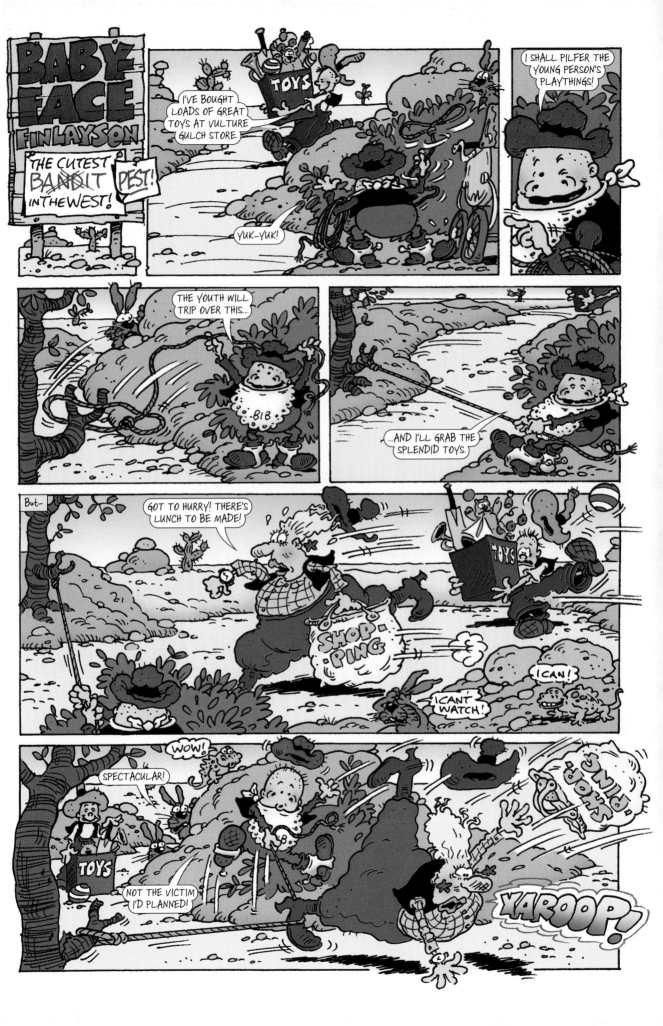

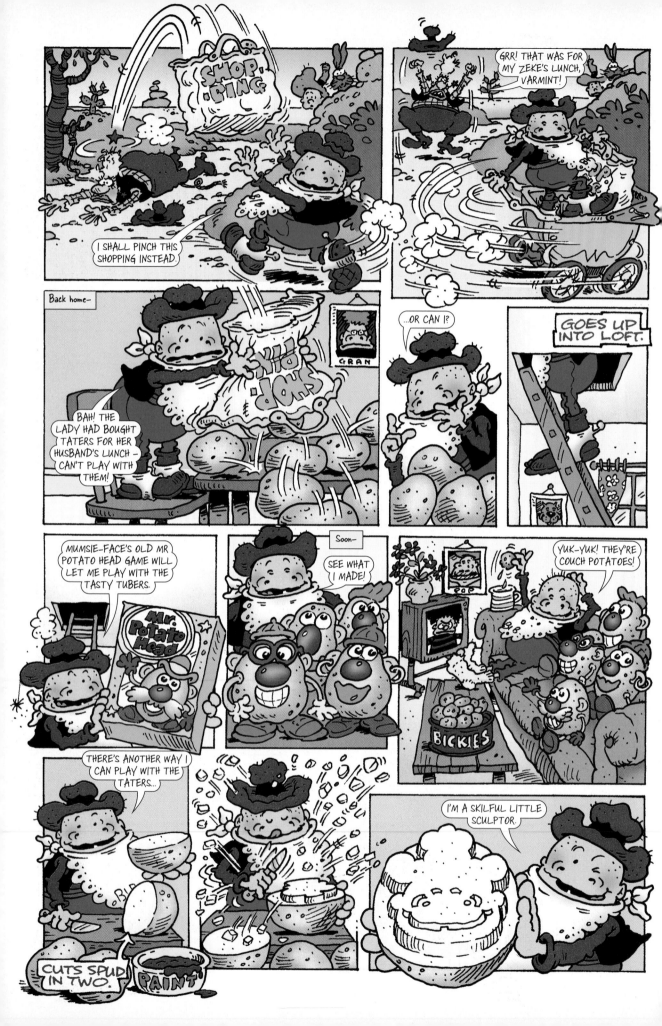

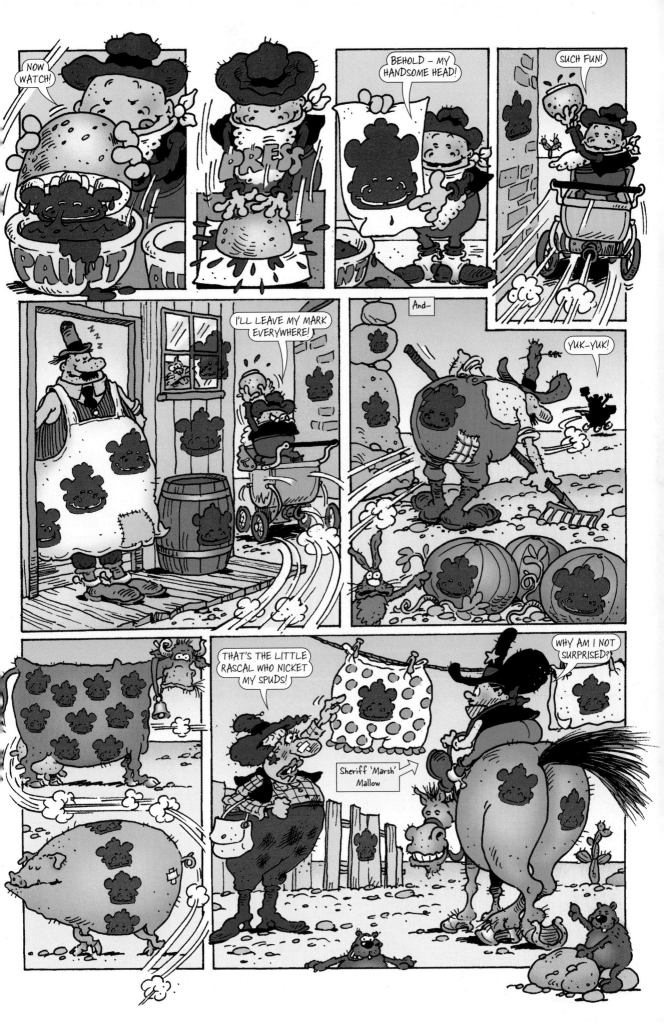

How to be a TATER-ARTIST and make your mark!

POTATO STAMPS

THEY'RE SPUDTASTIC!

An adult will need to help you cut out the potato stamp. You can design your own greeting cards, wrapping paper or even t-shirts with the correct sort of paint. Happy stamping!

YOU WILL NEED -

SMALL SHARP KNIFE

PAINT

BIG SPUD

SHALLOW DISH

PAPER

TATER ART

2 You can now use this shape as a stamp. Put the paint in a shallow dish so you can dip the stamps in the paint...

If you are stamping paper, use poster paint. Use fabric paint for t-shirts. You can use as many colours as you want – just wash your stamp before dipping the new colour.

HERE'S WHAT YOU DO -

1 Wash the potato and cut it in half. On the cut face of the potato, carve a simple shape like a heart or a star.

Please ask an adult to help with the carving. Cut away the potato round the shape so that the shape you want sticks up about half a centimetre.

I ♥ BEANO

__ __ __ __ __

__ __ __ __ __

__ __ __ __

__ __ __ __ __

__ __ __ __ __

__ __ __ __

__ __ __ __

__ __ __ __

__ __ __ __

__ __ __ __

__ __ __ __ __

__ __ __ __

__ __ __ __

__ __ __ __ __

__ __ __ __

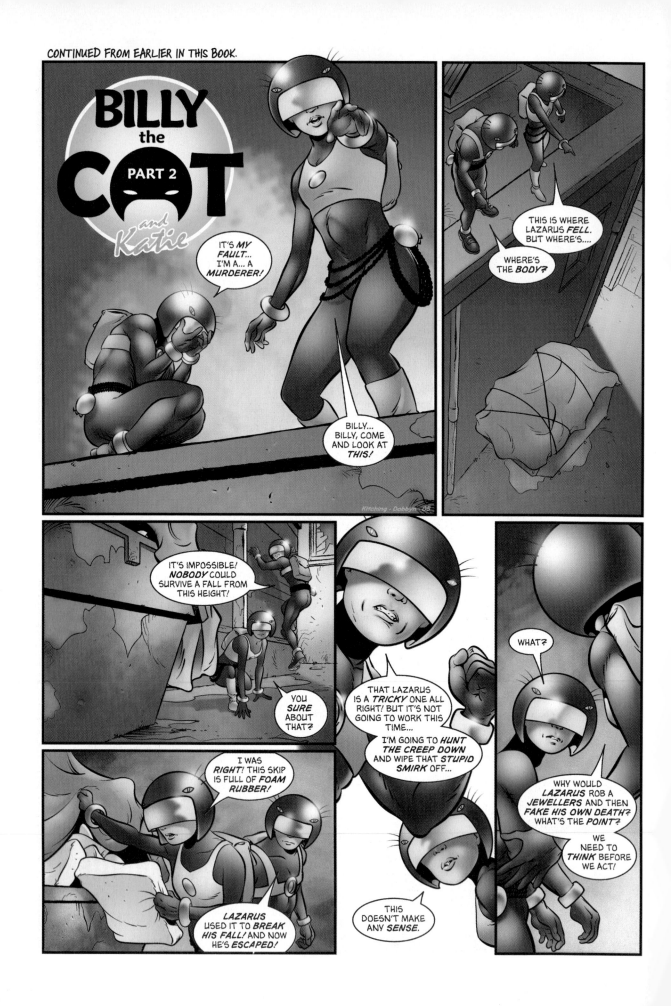

THIS IS *POINTLESS!* WE *KNOW* IT'S *SCOTT LAZARUS* WE WANT, WE SAW HIS *FACE!*

WHAT *MORE* DO WE NEED TO KNOW?

MICHAEL LAZARUS? WOULD YOU MIND ANSWERING A....

WHA? HOW DID YOU *FIND* ME?

GET LOST!

KRAK

KATIE, *NO!*

KATIE, ARE YOU?...

I'M *FINE* BILLY, THE *HELMET* TOOK THE IMPACT!

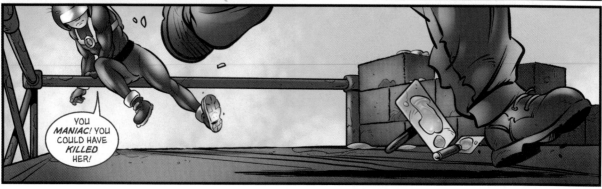

YOU *MANIAC!* YOU COULD HAVE *KILLED* HER!

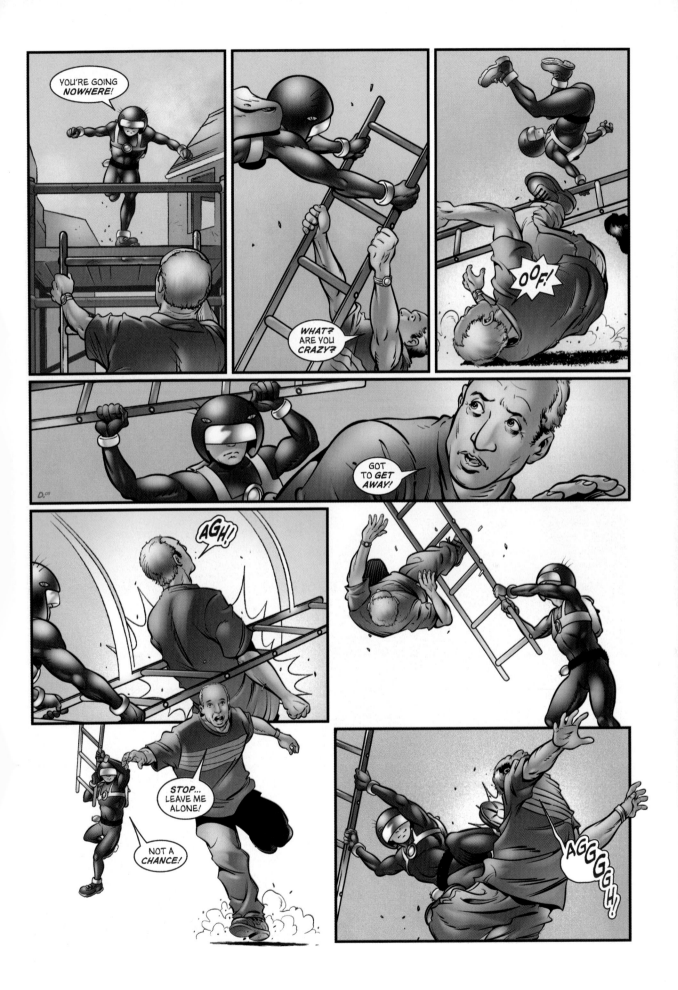

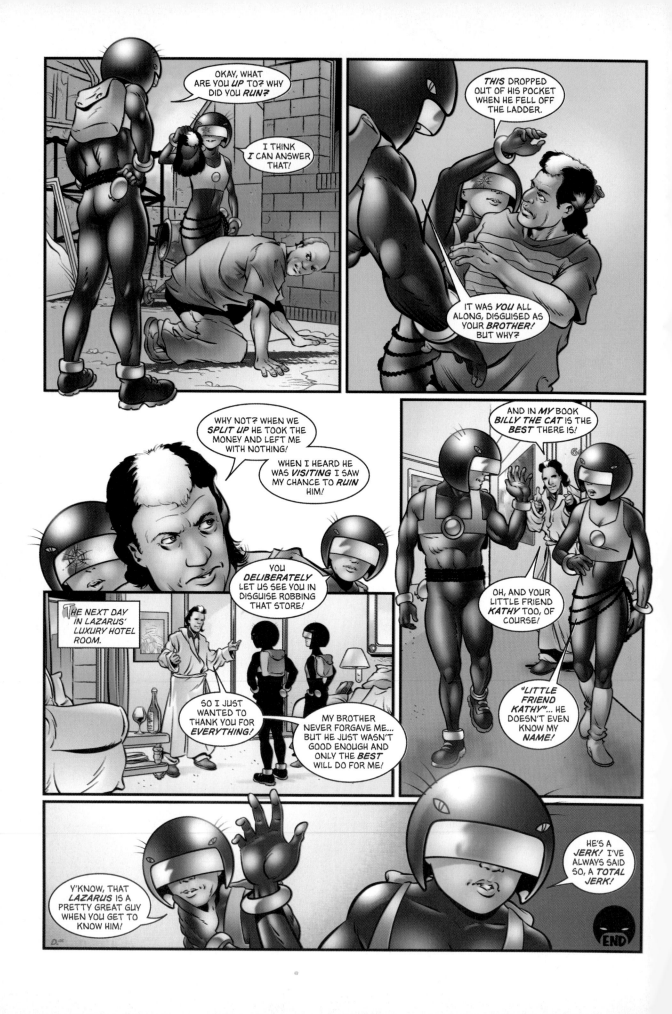

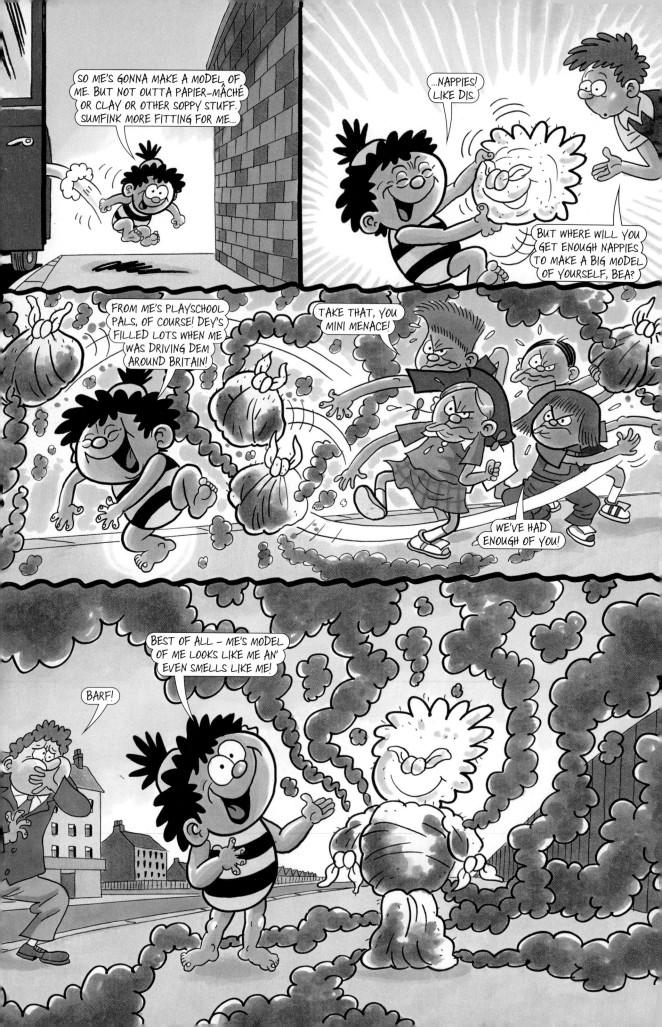

"BOXING NOT SO CLEVER!"

THE END